EGMONT
We bring stories to life

First published in Great Britain in 2020 by Egmont Books UK Ltd
2 Minster Court, 10th floor, London EC3R 7BB
www.egmontbooks.co.uk

Written by Dan Whitehead and Thomas McBrien
Edited by Thomas McBrien
Designed by Paul Lang and Andrea Philpots
Illustrations by Ryan Marsh
Production by Louis Harvey and Laura Grundy
Special thanks to Alex Wiltshire, Sherin Kwan, Filip Thoms, Amanda Ström, Kelsey Howard, Isabella Balk and Åsa Skogström
This book is an original creation by Egmont UK Limited

MOJANG

ISBN 978 1 4052 9639 7

70834/006
Printed in Italy

ONLINE SAFETY FOR YOUNGER FANS

Spending time online is great fun! Here are a few simple rules to help younger fans stay safe and keep the internet a great place to spend time:

- Never give out your real name – don't use it as your username.
- Never give out any of your personal details.
- Never tell anybody which school you go to or how old you are.
- Never tell anybody your password except a parent or a guardian.
- Be aware that you must be 13 or over to create an account on many sites. Always check the site policy and ask a parent or guardian for permission before registering.
- Always tell a parent or guardian if something is worrying you.

Stay safe online. Any website addresses listed in this book are correct at the time of going to print.
However, Egmont is not responsible for content hosted by third parties. Please be aware that online content can be subject to change and websites can contain content that is unsuitable for children. We advise that all children are supervised when using the internet.

Egmont takes its responsibility to the planet and its inhabitants very seriously.
We aim to use papers from well-managed forests run by responsible suppliers.

MOJANG

MINECRAFT

ANNUAL 2021

CONTENTS

8

34

65

HELLO! 7

IT'S BEEN A BUSY YEAR! 8

GAME OF THE DECADE 10

UN HABITAT: BLOCK BY BLOCK 12

POLLINATOR'S PARADISE BUILD CHALLENGE 14

THE NETHER 18

SPOT THE DIFFERENCE 20

MARKETPLACE 22

PILLAGER SURVIVAL CHALLENGE 26

VILLAGE LIFE 30

VILLAGE BUILD CHALLENGE 32

MINECRAFT DUNGEONS: THE TRAGEDY OF THE ARCH-ILLAGER 34

DUNGEON CRAWLERS 40

BUILDING HACKS 42

CHARACTER CREATOR 46

NOT ALL HEROES WEAR A CAPE 48

MINECRAFT EARTH 50

HOST A PIXEL PARTY CHALLENGE 52

BUILDERS & BIOMES 54

MINECRAFT HOUR OF CODE 56

PARKOUR PARK BUILD CHALLENGE 58

THE COOLEST COMMUNITY 62

CAMPFIRE TALES 64

DECIPHER THE ILLAGER 66

GOODBYE! 68

HELLO!

What, already?! Yes! It's time to welcome you to the Minecraft Annual 2021!

We've so much to share with you about all that's been happening across our blocky dimensions over the past year. Such as ... Minecraft Dungeons! An exciting new adventure which gives you a completely new way to journey through the Overworld! On the following pages, we've put together some secrets you can use to defeat the nefarious Arch-Illager.

And have you enjoyed exploring the strange and terrible new biomes of the Nether? We'll be taking you on a tour of their sights and introducing you to their new inhabitants. I've put on gold armour to make some tight new piglin friends, but I'm wondering why I decided to become a hoglin farmer.

One of the things we're most proud of is how Minecraft is active in the real world. Maybe you've been using Minecraft Earth to explore the streets and spaces near you? And there's also our Block by Block initiative with the United Nations – read all about how Minecraft is used to redesign and transform city space!

And look out for your chance to learn how to code ARTIFICIAL INTELLIGENCE with Minecraft! Wow, there's so much to see and do in this epic look back at another big year. I'd best shut up and let you dive right in!

Alex Wiltshire,

Mojang

IT'S BEEN A BUSY YEAR!

Minecraft has only grown more popular as it has gotten older. This year we've seen lots of exciting new content and loads of new mobs, blocks and biomes to explore and experience. That's not all: there's also a new board game and two new video games!

EXPERT GUIDE
WITH SPARKS

BUZZY BEES
Minecraft was buzzing with the arrival of these busy insects and their delicious honey.

LEFTOVERS!
You can now turn your leftover food and plants into useful bone meal.

A NEW DIMENSION
Minecraft Earth, a new augmented-reality mobile game, opened a new dimension of shared play.

AN EPIC QUEST
Minecraft Dungeons offered a whole new way to explore and go adventuring with friends.

BULLSEYE!
Lots of new blocks have been added to the game, like the new Target Block.

MAKEOVERS!
The new character creator allows you to craft your own personal avatar right down to the eyebrows.

GLOW FOR IT!
The Nether welcomed eerie new red and blue Netherwart Forests. Visit the new biomes to discover more.

CUBES!
Minecraft board game Builders and Biomes proved you don't need screens to have fun.

LIGHTS, CAMERA, ACTION!
Minecraft: The Movie was given a release date – in March 2022!

PIGLINS AND HOGLINS!
These tusky troublemakers arrived in the Nether. Piglins are easily distracted by shiny gold armour.

PILLAGERS!
Watch out for these crossbow-wielding mobs. They will smash villages and nick your best stuff!

THAT'S RETRO, DUDE!
To celebrate 10 years of Minecraft, Mojang released a browser edition remake of Minecraft Classic, taking us back to 2009 when all we had was 32 block types. To play, visit the Minecraft website and join up to 9 other players through your browser.

GAME OF THE DECADE
THANKS TO YOU, THE COMMUNITY

With every new block and mob added, the community explored and innovated to the delight of players and devs alike. From creating incredible redstone contraptions and breathtaking monuments to voting for new content, the players have been Minecraft's lifeblood since its inception. It has been a wild journey, but we wouldn't have it any other way. We hope you never change.

EXPERT GUIDE
WITH SPARKS

MORE THAN A GAME
Minecraft has become more than just a game. It's a platform, a social hub, a sandbox, an augmented reality. It is whatever you want it to be.

COMMUNITY OUTREACH
A game that brings together a supportive community is a special game indeed. Since its conception, Minecraft has worked with charitable organisations to raise awareness for global causes. Together, Minecrafters have launched a coral reef restoration project, raised donations for the WWF and rallied together for a 'Weekend for Water' livestream. What will the community do next? That's up to you to decide.

176 MILLION
COPIES SOLD

112 MILLION
UNIQUE MONTHLY USERS

100 BILLION
YOUTUBE VIEWS
Most watched game on YouTube in 2019

51%
of U.S. children aged 9-11 play Minecraft

NEW HORIZONS
Mojang has released two epic new games to the world of Minecraft. Check out Minecraft Earth and Minecraft Dungeons – guaranteed to provide hours of entertainment.

DEVICES
Minecraft has expanded to almost every desktop, mobile and console device available. Players can join their friends everywhere on their favourite devices.

AWARDS HIGHLIGHTS
It has been an incredible decade for Minecraft. Since its release, Minecraft has been named as one of the best, most influential and defining games of the decade by reviewers CNET, Business Insider, Entertainment Weekly, Polygon, TIME, WIRED, Eurogamer, Venturebeat, Washington Post and many more. Minecraft Earth was also recognised as one of TIME Magazine's Best Innovations of 2019!

EDUCATION
Minecraft Education has soared in recent years, with 35 million users playing the game in 115 countries. There are 500 free online lessons available, and since 2015 over 130 million hours of lessons have been completed by students around the globe.

UN HABITAT: BLOCK BY BLOCK

EXPERT GUIDE
WITH SCOUT

Have you ever been frustrated by how the cities around you are designed?

Are the shops too far away or the pavements too narrow? Marginalised communities around the world face problems just like these every day. Block by Block gets involved with these communities and works with them to improve their local area and redesign public spaces.

The foundation, a collaboration between Mojang, Microsoft and UN Habitat, has had wide success at getting people of all ages, backgrounds and education levels involved in local development projects. Through Minecraft, over 1.72 million people have been given a voice in shaping their communities, using the game as a platform to contribute and cooperate.

In less than a decade, Block by Block has funded and activated dozens of public space projects in over 30 countries. In 2019, 17 public space projects were completed, 36 additional public space projects were started and an astonishing 27 city-wide assessments for future projects completed.

WHY MINECRAFT?

Minecraft's sandbox style makes it easy for users of all ages to interact with and design their own builds. Block by Block uses the low-barrier game as an accessible tool for bringing people together from all areas of a community to help design how their public places will look. It provides a safe space that nurtures creativity and teamwork.

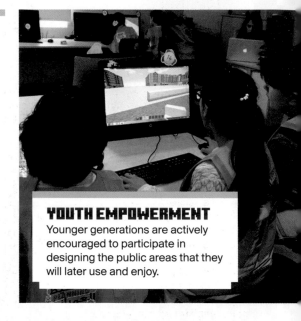

YOUTH EMPOWERMENT

Younger generations are actively encouraged to participate in designing the public areas that they will later use and enjoy.

ACCESSIBILITY

Block by Block work actively to involve people of all backgrounds and abilities to their workshops.

PROMOTING PEACE

Ambassadors host classes for refugees and community groups to promote peace and provide education on migrant, refugee and human rights.

SOCIAL INCLUSION

It's important for Block by Block that projects include everyone, especially poor people and women, whose voices are often not heard.

Every year,
Block by Block
receive hundreds
of applications from
communities wishing
to host a project in
their hometowns.

The Project Committee review the applications and evaluate projects based on suitability, sustainability and social impact. They select the projects that will have the greatest positive impact on the local communities and businesses.

KOSOVO

Kosovo is one of Europe's poorest countries and has a long history of conflict. In recent years, Kosovo's cities have seen rapid growth, sparking a need for well-designed public spaces. Block by Block joined up with the Municipality of Pristina in 2015 to design public spaces that can be enjoyed by everyone. Projects have since been completed in Sunny Hill and Mitrovica.

TRANSFORMING LIVES

Every Block by Block project aims to instil a sense of pride in the local communities. By encouraging a hands-on approach, the foundation sparks enthusiasm among the individuals who worked hard to revitalise their public spaces. Enthusiasm is contagious, all it takes is dedication. How can you help transform lives around you?

The initial project, Sunny Hill, saw the revitalisation of the largest and most populated public areas, creating a public space for 4000 local residents. In Mitrovica, the project brought together the residents of diverse communities that had historically been heavily divided. Newly created public spaces encouraged locals to interact and socialise with people outside of their own community. Through Minecraft, locals were finally able to see Mitrovica as one city.

VIETNAM

Hanoi, Vietnam is also experiencing rapid growth. Its centuries-old architecture has influenced the city design and resulted in a chaotic network of streets. Block by Block selected the Kim Chung neighbourhood as an area in need of special attention, as children were forced to commute to school through poorly lit, dangerous areas.

Block by Block organised a workshop with schoolgirls in the Kim Chung neighbourhood to analyse the area. The students were given an opportunity to address common problems of poor lighting, dark corners and heaped garbage. Working in teams, the students used Minecraft to reimagine the neighbourhood, creating an environment featuring increased lighting, improved signage and public restrooms. Addressing the issue of women's security, they also suggested shelters, security fences and free public phones. Their recommendations have sparked changes to how public spaces are developed.

POLLINATOR'S PARADISE BUILD CHALLENGE

PART 1

Bees help keep the natural world buzzing along, and now they do the same in Minecraft by pollinating plants and making delicious sticky honey! These colourful critters are great for speeding up crops. Are you ready to build your own horticultural haven?

BUILDING WITH MONTY

1 CROPS
Plant as many crops as you can. Bees will pollinate any plants they fly over while carrying pollen, making crops grow faster. Make sure you plant your crops between your hives and flowers for maximum coverage.

2 POLLEN
When a bee is loaded with pollen, you'll be able to see particles surrounding them. If you're looking for a bee's nest in the wild, you can follow a pollinated bee home to find out where it lives.

5 HONEY
Beehives and bee nests will fill with honey after five pollinating trips. Use an empty bottle to collect the delicious gooey goodness. Four bottles of honey will create a honey block that can slow down enemies if left on the ground. There's lots more you can do with this sticky treat!

6 BEEHIVES
Every beehive provides a cosy home for three bees. Plan how big your garden will be and then position lots of beehives around the outside.

3 CAMPFIRE
Place a campfire beneath a nest or in front of a hive to put the bees to sleep with the smoke. This lets you move them without being stung.

4 FLOWERS
Bees like flowers. Place them all around your garden to keep your bees pollinating. The more flowers in your garden, the busier your bees will be!

7 LOCATION, LOCATION, LOCATION!
Bees prefer mellow climates so pick a biome such as a flower forest for your garden. Have you ever seen a bee in the icy tundra? Nope!

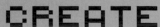
POLLINATOR'S PARADISE BUILD CHALLENGE

PART 2

BEE CAREFUL!
Just like real life, bees will sting you if you anger them, and if one bee attacks you then all their friends will too. Yikes! Any bee that stings will die, so play nicely!

SILK TOUCH
You can only move beehives and nests using a tool with a Silk Touch enchantment. Any other tool will destroy it – and anger the bees living inside!

GREENHOUSE CONSERVATORY STRUCTURE

⏱ **0.5 HRS**   ⬡⬡⬡⬡ **EASY**

BUILDING WITH MONTY

Bees are the latest way to grow crops fast, but the old ways still work great too. Build a greenhouse around your Pollinator's Paradise garden for the best of both worlds!

BUILD TIP

Your greenhouse doesn't need sunlight to grow plants. Add some lanterns to light up the interior so your plants can keep growing through the night. Let the bees get some rest!

Birch stairs

9 blocks

Lantern

Birch trapdoor

Black stained glass pane

9 blocks

6 blocks

16 blocks

Mossy cobblestone

17

THE NETHER

Another major update has hit the main stage, this time overhauling our favourite dimension! There are lots of new mobs and blocks and even entire new biomes to discover. Let's dive into the portal and discover what's new in the Nether.

EXPERT GUIDE
WITH SCOUT

SOULSAND VALLEY

Look out for Soulsand Valley, with its expansive lava lakes, deep ravines and tall basalt towers. This biome has a light blue glow and little grey particles floating in the air. It's a popular hotspot for ghasts and skeletons, so make sure to pack a ranged weapon and some arrows!

CRIMSON FOREST

This new biome is a fungi haven. Visit this dark red forest to find crimson items, like shroomlights and weeping vines. Watch out, the hostile piglins and aggressive hoglins have made it their home. Bring some bone meal to grow the fungi – the results are spectacular!

BASALT TOWER

SHROOMLIGHT

NETHER FOSSILS

FUNGI

PIGLINS

Piglins are hostile mobs, unless you're wearing gold armour. Then they'll happily trade with you! You will need to make the first move. Be careful, they're easily provoked. Drop a gold ingot at their feet to start bartering.

ANCIENT DEBRIS

WARPED FORESTS

This is the most peaceful place in the Nether. It's absolutely packed with huge warped fungi, shroomlights and warped nylium. Head over to this dark blue biome to get all your warped supplies! Keep an eye out for the endermen – they love it here. Bring a pumpkin.

NETHERITE

Attention all survivalists! Word has reached us of a new rare and mysterious material more durable than diamond. Known as netherite, this substance has some special properties and can be used to improve diamond items. Forge an ingot of netherite using 4 netherite scraps and 4 gold ingots.

NETHERITE INGOT RECIPE

CRIMSON NYLIUM

WEEPING VINES

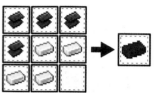

AWARD

This year we've decided to nominate our choice for the most difficult and time-consuming item in the game: the netherite hoe. You will need two of the rarest blocks in the game to create just one! Like other netherite items, the netherite hoe will float in lava but unlike other netherite items, it is not more efficient than diamond hoes. It takes a lot of time and effort to create this item.

HOGLINS

Hoglins are aggressive on sight and will use their powerful horns to fling players into the air. They can be bred using crimson fungi, making them the only hostile mob you can farm in the Nether, but they despise warped fungi. Watch your fingers!

SOUL FIRE

NEW BLOCKS AND ITEMS

SOUL TORCH & LANTERN

WARPED WOOD

CRIMSON WOOD

ANCIENT DEBRIS

BASALT

NETHERITE INGOTS

SOUL SOIL

SPOT THE DIFFERENCE

Exploring new biomes is great fun! There are so many new blocks and mobs to discover. It's important that you pay attention to detail to make sure you find everything a new biome has to offer. Let's put your observation skills to the test! Can you spot the ten differences between these two pictures?

CHALLENGE TIME
WITH BEAR

Tick off the differences as you find them ...

1 ⬡ 2 ⬡ 3 ⬡ 4 ⬡ 5 ⬡

6 ⬡ 7 ⬡ 8 ⬡ 9 ⬡ 10 ⬡

Check your answers on page 68.

MARKETPLACE

Visit the Marketplace to find skins, textures, worlds and mash-ups made by the amazing community creators across all of the Bedrock platforms. There are countless packs available to choose from and lots of new exciting content to experience. Let's take a look at some of our favourites.

EXPERT GUIDE WITH SPARKS

ADVENTURE MAPS

Experience epic and exciting adventures as you immerse yourself in the world of Minecraft with these packs.

HARDCORE ISLAND
BY EVERBLOOM

Take hardcore to the next level! Survive 7 days on a mystical island. One death and it's all over. Can you solve the mystery and leave the island, or will you be stuck here with me forever?

RAGE PARKOUR
BY THE RAGE CRAFT ROOM

Unleash your competitive side as you race with friends, dodging obstacles and navigating hazards on the way to the finish line. First to complete all 33 levels wins eternal bragging rights.

DUCKTALES
BY MINECRAFT

From McDuck Manor to Mount Neverrest, this adventure is absolutely quackers! We loved discovering the history of Duckberg, along with all its mysteries and unique puzzles.

JUNGLE EXPLORERS
BY 4J STUDIOS

Full of ancient tombs, dangerous animals and deadly traps, trekking through this jungle felt like stepping into the wild. Grab this pack to discover the secrets hidden among the trees.

TEXTURE PACKS

Check out these cool texture packs to give your Minecraft experience a refreshing new look!

CLASSIC TEXTURE
BY MINECRAFT

The classic Minecraft texture we all know and love! Join us as we go retro and return to Minecraft's roots with this classic texture pack. I'm feeling nostalgic already.

PUREBDCRAFT
BY BDCRAFT

Get ready to embrace your inner geek. Travel to a cartoon world where everything is completely recreated with a comic-book flavour. Finding geeky references is just the start of the fun.

FROZEN
BY MINECRAFT

Visit Anna, Elsa, Olaf and friends in this Frozen-themed world! Join us as we play mini-games and complete puzzles, all while singing along to our favourite Frozen songs.

SIMPLY CUBED
BY PIXEL²

The creators of this pack had one goal in mind – and they nailed it! Simply Cubed is clean, elegant and guaranteed to liven up your builds with its vivid colours and unique designs.

STEAMPUNK
BY MINECRAFT

Feeling industrious? Our favourite dystopian Victorian era style pack will make your industrial world stand out with wonderful textures and retro-futuristic outfits.

STONE AGE
BY POLYMAPS

Your first day in Minecraft will never be the same again. Discover fire, build shelters and grow the first farms in an ancient world full of cave drawings and long-extinct species.

MARKETPLACE

⬡ SURVIVAL WORLDS

Looking for a real challenge? Check out these survival worlds and see how long you can last.

JEWEL OF THE DESERT
BY SHALIQUINN'S SCHEMATICS

Nestled in the harsh desert sands lies an ancient city and its monuments. Explore the mysteries left behind, visit the pyramids and build a kingdom with a sphinx on its doorstep.

ARCTIC ANIMALS
BY VAERON

Attention animal lovers! Befriend penguins, ride a woolly mammoth and discover the arctic on an expedition vessel with this cute new animal pack. There's lots of fun new outfits too!

CHICKEN BLOCK
BY NETHERPIXEL

Try out our favourite sky challenge yet! Survive high up in the sky with the help of some very special chickens. With limited resources, this is a Skyblock challenge with a poultry twist.

MOUSE HOUSE
BY POLYMAPS

Roleplay as a cheese-loving, trap-hating little mouse! Explore the family home, fight off creepy-crawlies and avoid the sewer rats as you set out in search for some tasty, smelly cheese!

BEEHIVE
BY CUBECRAFT GAMES

Be the happiest bee you can be in this wonderful Beehive world. Take a trip to the honeycomb caves and and get lost among giant flower fields, all while riding your very own bee!

MASH-UPS

Can't decide what you want? Check out these mash-up packs containing everything you need to totally transform your world.

STEVEN UNIVERSE
BY MINECRAFT

Join half-Gem hero Steven and his trio of friends as they enter the Minecraft universe. Fight monsters, eat breakfast and visit your favourite locations. We'll always save the day!

MAYAN LEGENDS
BY CYCLONE DESIGNS

Travel back thousands of years to the time of the Mayans. Put your survival skills to the test as you discover the beauty of an ancient civilisation and search for lost treasure in this exotic Mayan-themed mash-up.

DEEP SEA
BY CYCLONE DESIGNS

Grab your scuba gear, take a big breath and get ready to dive down to the deepest depths! Visit an underwater city, meet strange new creatures and embark on a submarine cruise in this underwater world.

TOY STORY
BY MINECRAFT

Open the toy box and join Woody, Buzz Lightyear and the rest of the gang as they come to life in this mash-up adventure! Be a part of the action as they navigate the dangers of being toys in the real world.

ANIMAL KINGDOM MASH-UP
BY CYCLONE DESIGNS

If you're an animal lover like me, you're going to love this animal kingdom mash-up. Packed with detailed biomes, epic dungeons and lots of unique new animal mobs and skins, this pack makes exploring a feel like a safari.

PILLAGER SURVIVAL CHALLENGE

PART 1

CHALLENGE TIME WITH SCOUT

Put your combat skills to the ultimate test by surviving a pillager raid. Defend the village and reap the rewards, but only if you can defeat wave after wave of fiendish attackers! Reckon you're up to it? Sharpen your sword and find out!

1 First things first: You're going to need weapons and armour. A diamond sword and diamond armour are essential, and you're going to want a strong shield and a bow as well. If you don't have all of these, you're in for a tough battle ahead!

2 Be prepared! You'll need every advantage. A sword enchanted with sharpness and armour enchanted with protection could save your life. Unbreaking enchantments are even better!

3 You're going to take damage – yikes! – so make sure to stock up with lots of bread to top up your health. Golden apples will be a huge help too, and having some milk handy will be useful to get rid of any nasty status effects in battle!

4 If you plan ahead, you can fortify the village before starting the raid. Raiders cannot break blocks, so cobblestone or even wooden walls are great for keeping them at a safe distance.

5 You don't have to fight alone. Iron golems like nothing more than scrapping with pillagers, so if the village doesn't already have one, create your own to assist you in battle.

6 You'll lose the raid if all the villagers die, so keep them safe! Ring the village bell to send them to their houses. You can block the doors with cobblestone to keep raiders out. All part of the service!

7 Raids comes in waves of 3 on easy mode, 5 on normal mode and 7 on hard mode. Each wave gets tougher as the raid continues, with enemy witches and evokers joining the fight. The raid is only won when they're all defeated, so keep an eye on the raid bar at the top of the screen and always keep track of what's still to come.

Number of mobs in each wave (Bedrock Edition)							
MOBS	1	2	3	4	5	6	7
Pillager	4	3		3		5	
Vindicator		2			4	2	6
Ravager			1		1		
Witch				3		1	1
Evoker					1		2
Ravager + Pillager					1		1
Ravager + Evoker							1

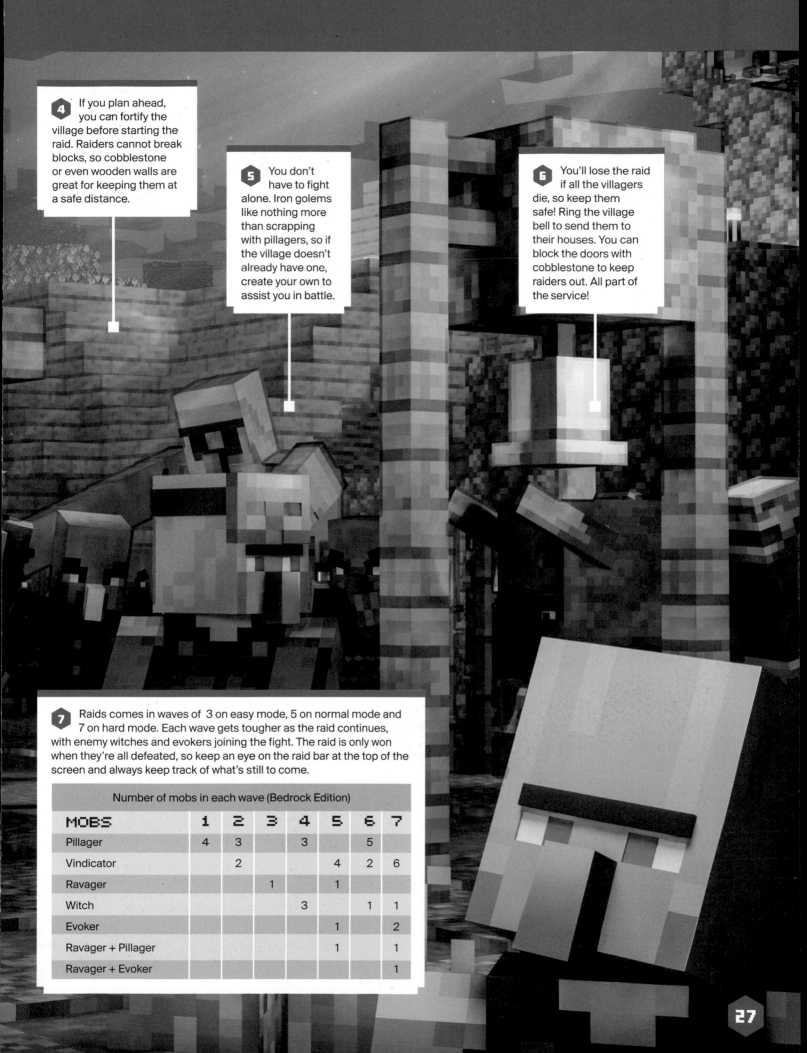

PILLAGER SURVIVAL CHALLENGE

PART 2

WATCH OUT FOR WITCHES!

Raids on harder difficulties will introduce evokers and witches to the foray. Evokers will summon vexes to assist, while witches will throw potions that cause harmful status effects. Drink your bucket of milk now!

READY? FIGHT!

So how do you start a raid? First of all you need to have the bad omen status effect. You get this by killing an illager captain – you can't miss 'em, they're the ones in outposts and on patrol with banners above their heads. With the bad omen active, walk into a village and the raid will begin.

KNOW YOUR ENEMY!

Early waves of raid mobs will consist of crossbow-wielding pillagers and vindicators with iron axes. Watch out for the ravagers though – these headbutting beasts do serious damage, especially if they have a rider. Stay out of their way!

FIRE 'EM UP!

Are you struggling? Keep getting defeated in Raids? Psst, here's a sneaky tip – don't forget you can load crossbows with fireworks for an explosive surprise. That should help you turn the tables on those pesky raiders!

TOP TIP!

Here's a cool little secret for you! Place a dispenser next to a villager and you can use it to give them armour. It won't show up on their body, unless it's a pumpkin or mob head, but they'll still get the protective benefits, and that includes any enchantments. Very handy!

VICTORY!

Yay! You've survived the raid and defeated the pillagers! The grateful villagers will throw a celebration in your honour, and you'll get a trading discount from them for a short time afterwards. If you're playing Java Edition, they'll even throw gifts at you! Cheers mate!

VILLAGE LIFE

Exploring by yourself is great fun, but sometimes you just want some company. That's where villagers come in! Villagers are useful NPC characters that can help you out in-game. These friendly folks can be really useful if you treat them nicely, so get ready to shake some hands – it's time to meet the neighbours!

EXPERT GUIDE
WITH SPARKS

BABY VILLAGER

Aaaw! They're so cute! Baby villagers will chase each other around the village and love jumping on their beds. They can't trade with you – they're babies! – but they're fun to watch as they dash around, popping in and out of all the houses without even knocking. After only 20 minutes they'll become adults. What a swizz! Think of all those missed birthdays!

THE FOOD OF LOVE!

Villagers have eight personal inventory slots, which they fill with the bread, carrots, potatoes, wheat, beetroot and seeds they find. A full inventory is important for breeding, so make sure the villagers can find lots of food!

ADULT VILLAGER

Villagers will go about their business and make themselves useful, but you can steer them toward jobs by placing job blocks inside the village boundaries. Unemployed villagers will seek out job blocks and get to work. You can trade with employed villagers to get useful items – including some items you cannot find by yourself.

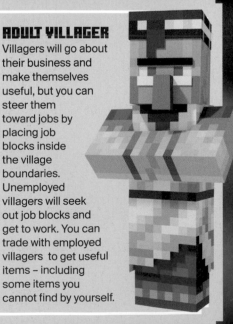

HOME COMFORTS!

Villagers like to stay close to home. If they stray outside of the village boundaries, they hurry back inside. A villager who travels more than 32 blocks away from their village will forget where they live! Doh!

SHINY!

Villagers use emeralds as currency, and the quickest way to stock up on these gems is to trade with an armourer or tool smith. They'll both gladly swap blocks of dirty old coal for shiny new emeralds. Sweet deal!

SWAPSIES!

Villagers will happily trade with you, unless you've attacked them, offering different items depending on their profession. They will level up each time you trade, unlocking better deals and rare items, so be generous!

CHATTER-BOXES!

Villagers love to gossip! They'll gather around the village bell to talk about you, so be aware that any good deeds – or bad – will affect your reputation and trading prices with the whole village!

ZOMBIE VILLAGER

If you're playing on normal or hard mode, when a zombie attacks a villager, the villager may then become a zombie villager. While in this state it'll behave like a normal zombie, but can pick up and use armour and weapons. Zombie villagers can also swim underwater without dying. The only cures for zombie villagers are golden apples, tipped arrows and splash potions of weakness. Once cured, the villager will give you a big discount on any trades as a thank-you!

WANDERING TRADER

Keep your eyes open for this cool dude in blue! There's only ever one of them in the world at a time, strolling around with their pet llamas. They always have up to 6 useful trades on offer. You'll only see them during the daytime though – the trader turns invisible at night! If you attack the wandering trader it will run away while its llamas pelt you with spit!

JOB BLOCKS

Need a specific villager type to trade with? Use this list to find out which job block you'll need …

BLAST FURNACE
Armourer

SMOKER
Butcher

CARTOGRAPHY TABLE
Cartographer

BREWING STAND
Cleric

COMPOSTER
Farmer

BARREL
Fisherman

CAULDRON
Leatherworker

LECTERN
Librarian

FLETCHING TABLE
Fletcher

SMITHING TABLE
Toolsmith

GRINDSTONE
Weaponsmith

LOOM
Shepherd

STONE CUTTER
Stone Mason

VILLAGE BUILD CHALLENGE

It's one thing to build a house, but building an entire village? That's the mark of a true Minecrafter! Let's build our very own custom village together!

EXPERT GUIDE WITH SPARKS

1 Start by picking a spot that is nice and safe. Villagers aren't that bright and will easily wander off cliffs or slip into hot lava. Wall off the area you want to use to keep dangerous mobs out and healthy villagers in.

3 Villagers are much more useful when they have a job! Place a composter block inside the village and an unemployed villager will use it to become a farmer. The farmer will then grow food for everyone. That's really important!

2 Villagers will need homes and beds to stay in. Construct some homes within the confines of your village and make sure to add doorways and beds for the villagers. These homes can be as large or as small as you like. Why not create some larger houses for growing families?

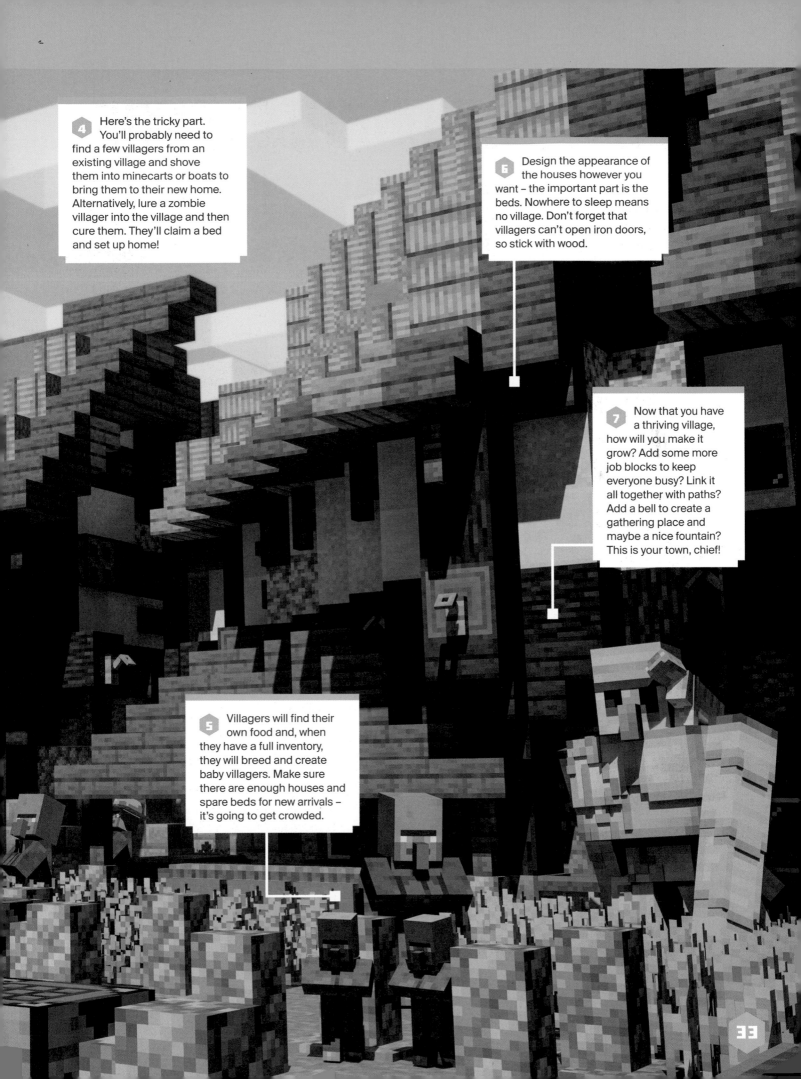

4 Here's the tricky part. You'll probably need to find a few villagers from an existing village and shove them into minecarts or boats to bring them to their new home. Alternatively, lure a zombie villager into the village and then cure them. They'll claim a bed and set up home!

6 Design the appearance of the houses however you want – the important part is the beds. Nowhere to sleep means no village. Don't forget that villagers can't open iron doors, so stick with wood.

7 Now that you have a thriving village, how will you make it grow? Add some more job blocks to keep everyone busy? Link it all together with paths? Add a bell to create a gathering place and maybe a nice fountain? This is your town, chief!

5 Villagers will find their own food and, when they have a full inventory, they will breed and create baby villagers. Make sure there are enough houses and spare beds for new arrivals – it's going to get crowded.

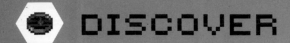

MINECRAFT DUNGEONS:
THE TRAGEDY OF THE ARCH-ILLAGER

Minecraft Dungeons is a brand new hack-and-slash adventure set in the world of Minecraft. Join forces with your friends as you set out to defeat the Arch-Illager and free the land from his evil cohorts. You'll fight evil mobs, scoop up loot and uncover secrets as you get closer and closer to ending the Arch-Illager's reign of terror. Are you ready for a challenge?

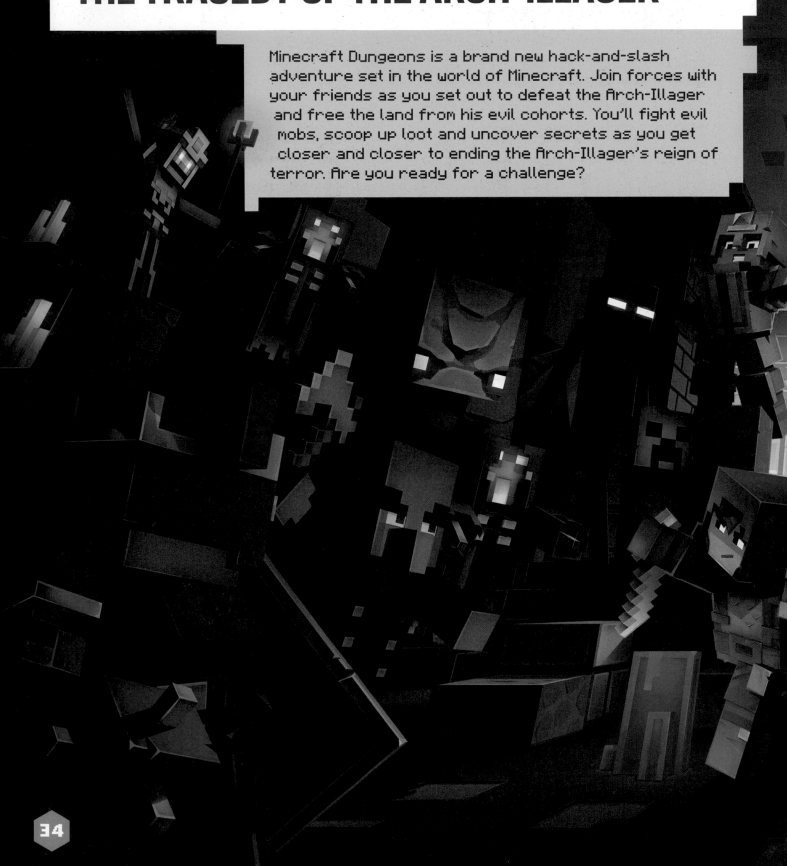

IT WAS A TIME OF GREAT ADVENTURE ... AND DANGER.

Shunned by his kin, an Illager wandered the land, seeking a new home. But all he found was hatred. Driven by rage against those who wronged him, he wandered blind to whatever end. Until at long last, the Illager found something that would change him forever ...

THE ORB OF DOMINANCE.

Corrupted by evil, driven by vengeance, the Arch-Illager made all bow before him. If they did not bow, they would fall and so the Illagers raided the land.

Who would have the valour, the purity of heart, to stand against the Arch-Illager's reign of terror?

MAYBE ... YOU?

DUNGEONS – GAMEPLAY

PART 1

The Arch-Illager and his forces have invaded the land. Displaced villagers need you to travel to Squid Coast and free them. Grab your weapons and get ready to embark on a quest of epic proportions as you set out to face the Arch-Illager and his army of despicable minions in this new dungeon adventure video game.

EXPERT GUIDE WITH SCOUT

MULTIPLAYER

Join forces with fellow warriors as you charge into the fray. Play to each of your strengths and find out who is most worthy of the challenge.

DIFFERENT PLAYSTYLE

Whether you like to charge into battle like a tank, shoot arrows from above like an archer or harness the magical elements like a mage, there is a playstyle to suit everyone's preferences.

VILLAINOUS INVADERS

Terrible new abominations have allied themselves with the Arch-Illager. These mobs are the vilest in the land, capable of unknown horrors. Keep an eye out for these monstrosities as you venture deep into the Arch-Illagers territory.

FRIENDLY FACES

Recognise these friendly mobs? Chased away by the Arch-Illager's forces, these mobs are the companions of heroes and will offer their assistance to those in need.

OLD THREATS

Face down your favourite mobs as you charge the hordes of skeletons, zombies, spiders and jockeys that have joined forces with the Arch-Illager.

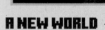

A NEW WORLD

Travel to Squid Coast to begin your journey. The Arch-Illager rules over his domain from the ramparts of the Obsidian Pinnacle, but to reach him you must traverse his occupied lands and defeat the mobs sent to stop you in your tracks.

LOOT

Defeat mobs and pick up loot. Upgrade your weapons and equipment as you collect useful items to aid your progress.

CONSUMABLES

Collect consumable boosts to aid you on your journey!

DUNGEONS – GAMEPLAY

PART 2

COOLDOWNS
Use special moves and abilities to defeat stronger opponents. Keep an eye on cooldowns to avoid getting caught.

SMASHABLES
Smash pots and containers to find emeralds and consumables.

HOTKEYS
Keep your three best Artifacts active at all times.

ARTIFACTS
Search for rare and powerful Artifacts to aid you on your journey.

OBJECTIVES
Follow markers and complete objectives to advance to the next level.

UNDEAD FORCES
Battle through hordes of undead zombies and skeletons that block the path.

CONSUMABLES
Food and potions provide immediate support for a short period of time.

HEALTH POTION
Watch your health bar! Chug a health potion when it gets low.

EMERALDS
Collect emeralds to upgrade weapons and equipment as you progress.

65

E   M   50

Lv 14

DUNGEON CRAWLERS

Bear has returned from the Obsidian Pinnacle with tales of the Arch-Illagers evil doings. Upon seeing the terrible challenge that lay ahead, Bear decided to create this exercise to prepare future dungeon adventurers. Will you be the first to reach the end?

CHALLENGE TIME WITH BEAR

36

37
A Key Golem opens a new path for you! *Move forward one space!*

38

35
A spawner blocks the path. *Miss a turn.*

34

33
You find a shortcut! *Roll again!!*

32

18
Urk! A zombie got you! *Go back to the start!*

19

20
Nice! You found some Emeralds! *Roll again!*

21
What's that noise? *Run forward two spaces just in case!*

17

16

15

14
You find an Enchanted Apple in a chest! *Move forward five spaces!*

13

START

1

2

3
A torch lights your way! *Move forward three spaces!*

END

44
Your torch has gone out! **Miss a turn!**

39
An obsidian wall blocks the way! *Miss a turn!*

40
A friendly merchant leads the way. *Move forward three spaces!*

41

42

43

30

31
Your health bar is low! *Miss a turn!*

29

28

27
Oh no! A skeleton! *Run back four spaces!*

22

23

24
Yuck, cobwebs! You're stuck! *Miss a turn!*

25
You find a Feather! *Jump ahead three spaces!*

26

12
You trip on a rock! *Go back one space!*

11

10
Glug! A Potion of Swiftness. *Roll again!*

9
You find a Great Hammer! *Clobber your way forward two spaces!*

4

5
You lost your bearings! *Move back three spaces!*

6

7

8
Yikes! A spider! *Run back four spaces!*

BUILDING HACKS

PART 1

Are you ready to take your builds to the next level? Becoming a top Minecraft creator takes patience, skill and a lot of imagination. Follow our expert top tips and soon your builds will blow people's socks off!

BUILDING WITH MONTY

CHANGE THE WORLD!

If you want to master big builds then you need to start terraforming. That means shaping the landscape to suit what you want to build. Don't be afraid to flatten hills and fill in valleys! The best creators don't get rid of all the natural features but instead work them into their design to make something truly impressive!

ROUNDED BUILDINGS

TERRAFORMED LANDSCAPE

DON'T FEAR SPHERES!

Everything in Minecraft is square, obviously! So how do you make round objects, like circles and spheres? It's easier than you think. To make rings, follow these diagrams. Turn the rings into a sphere by making a series of rings, each slightly larger than the last. Repeat the process going from large to small to make the other half. Want a bigger sphere? Just scale up the size of the rings!

5x5

7x7

9x9

11x11

11x11

BUILDING HACKS

PART 2

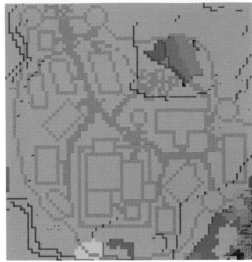

THINK AHEAD!

Always plan your big builds carefully. Use squared graph paper if you need to. Once you've got a clear space in your biome, lay out the shape of your construction using lines of blocks. This will help you stay on design as you progress through your build.

REACH NEW HEIGHTS!

Need to get to the top of a tall building project? Just use scaffolding! You can build tall towers of this useful block type while still standing on the ground. Then by jumping and crouching you can quickly move up and down to reach different areas of your build. When you're finished, just destroy the bottom block and the whole structure collapses down, leaving you with your completed masterpiece!

LIGHT IT UP!

Torches are really useful but look pretty basic for advanced builds. Luckily they're not the only light source. Did you know that carpet tiles let light through? They do! Build a glowstone floor then lay your fanciest carpet design on top. Bingo! Instant mood lighting with no torches in sight.

EMBRACE VARIETY!

Buildings that are made from all the same blocks look really boring! Mix things up a bit – throw some mossy cobblestone in with the normal cobblestone, or add wooden windowsills and other features. Look at real life buildings and study all the shapes, colours and textures! The limit is your imagination.

FIREPROOFING!

Want to keep your build safe from ravaging flames, but also include some nice wooden features in the design? Use wooden trapdoors instead of normal planks! They still look stylish but did you know they can't catch fire? It's true!

CHARACTER CREATOR

Everyone loves character skins. Guess what? Now you can completely choose the way you look. That's right, the Character Creator has opened up a whole new way to get creative in Bedrock and Minecraft Earth. Let's check out our favourite features!

DRESSING UP
WITH MONTY

GET SOME COLOUR!

Want to match your real-life skin tone? Use the Base tab, then open the paint palette to change your skin to dark or light brown, pink or even blue, yellow or bright green!

ARMED AND READY!

You can now change the design of both your arms and both legs. You can even give your Minecraft avatar a prosthetic limb.

TIME FOR A TRIM?

There are over 30 free hair styles you can choose from, including spikes, ponytails and even bald heads. I can't decide between an afro or a curly bob! Which do you think suits me best?

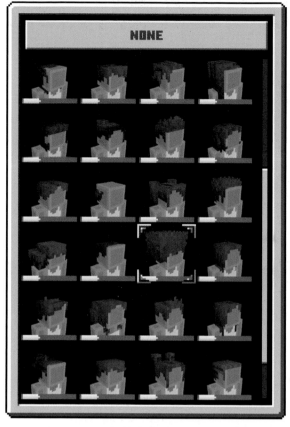

NONE

LOOK OUT!

Eyes front! You can really change the way you look with different eyes. Why not go super cute with the Delighted Gaze or scare everyone away with the Steely Stare!

NONE

GROWING UP!

There are four different heights to choose from on the Size tab, so be as big or small as you like! You'll still be two blocks tall in the game though, so you won't have to redesign all your doorways.

IN A FLAP!

Don't forget – if you've got any capes from attending MineCon events or have downloaded the Founders Cape from the Marketplace, you can apply them to any custom body you make in the Character Creator. Swish!

47

NOT ALL HEROES WEAR A CAPE

Wow, look at the size of this dressing room! I bet there must be every single item in the game in those chests. There's so much choice I can't decide what I like! Hey, maybe you can help me design some outfits? I'll need one for exploring and one for building.

CHALLENGE TIME
WITH BEAR

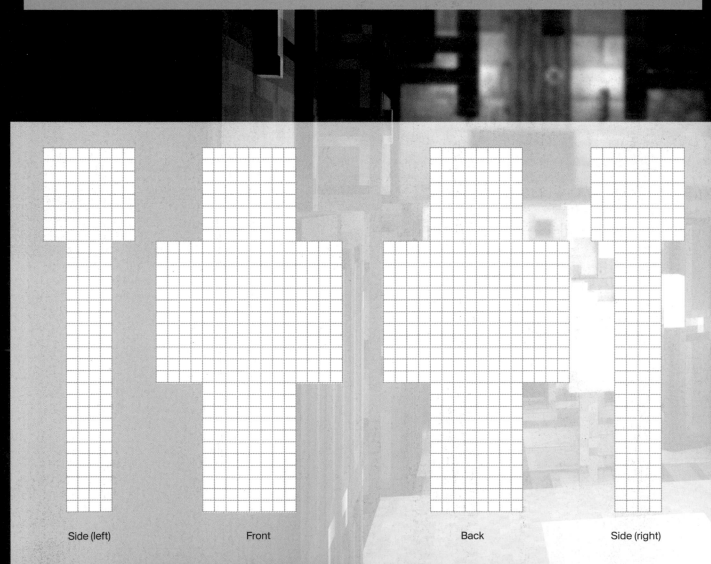

Side (left)   Front   Back   Side (right)

Side (left)

Front

Back

Side (right)

MINECRAFT EARTH

BUILDING
WITH SPARKS

Ever wished you could see your best Minecraft creations in real life? Well, in Minecraft Earth you can! This augmented reality, or AR, game lets you gather resources while walking around and use them to create amazing builds that can be made to appear in your garden, park or wherever you want! And best of all, you can do all of this with friends! What are you waiting for? Get tapping!

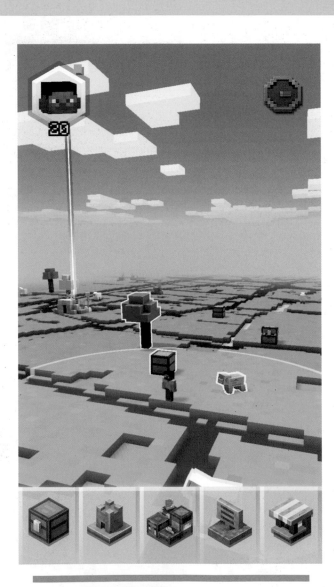

EXPLORE AND TAP!

Whenever you walk anywhere, scenery, chests and mobs will spawn on the Minecraft Earth map. These are called tappables, so you know what to do! Tap 'em to start filling up your inventory with all the resources you can find!

BE ADVENTUROUS!

Keep an eye open for Adventures. These are easy to spot with their beacon of light shooting up in the air. Tap the icon, place it in the real world with your camera to get the Adventure started, then invite your friends to join as you collect resources, uncover cool secrets and battle enemy mobs!

RISE TO THE CHALLENGE!

Always check the Challenges tab. You will be constantly rewarded for tapping and crafting, so pay attention to what you should collect. Completing these is the best way to level-up fast.

PATIENCE PAYS OFF!

A stone pickaxe takes five minutes to craft, so use your fists until it's ready and always keep a spare for when it breaks.

THINK OUTSIDE THE BLOCKS!

Some Adventures will include simple puzzles or tasks, such as placing flower pots on matching tiles. Solve the puzzle, collect better loot!

HOST A PIXEL PARTY CHALLENGE

They say that many hands make light work, so let's put that to the test with an epic build challenge. Fancy adding a Minecraft Earth skyscraper to the street where you live? Of course you do! It'll take lots of resources and lots of co-operation though. Are you and your mates up to the task? Let's find out!

BUILDING WITH SPARKS

1 MAKE FRIENDS!

Pixel parties are better with friends, so get all your mates to download Minecraft Earth and scan your in-game QR code to join you online. Only people who are invited can work on a buildplate and make permanent changes. Any blocks you and your friends contribute will be left on the build when you exit.

2 STOCK UP ON EVERYTHING!

This is going to be a mammoth build so load up your inventories, gather the gang together and go walking. Collect tappables and mine everything you can from Adventures. You'll need to pool all your resources together, so everyone should be collecting as much as they can before starting to build.

3 GET A BIG PLATE!

No, not for dinner. A buildplate! This is where you construct your creations in Minecraft Earth. The largest available plate is 32×32. You'll gain access to larger plates as you level up and you can buy them from the store using rubies collected in-game. All plates have the same height limit – 221 blocks – so even the smallest plate can hold a big build!

THINK LIKE AN ARCHITECT!

Anyone can build a giant grey stone tower, so what design flourishes can you add to the outside to make it more visually interesting? For an extra challenge, how about adding stairs inside that go all the way to the top?

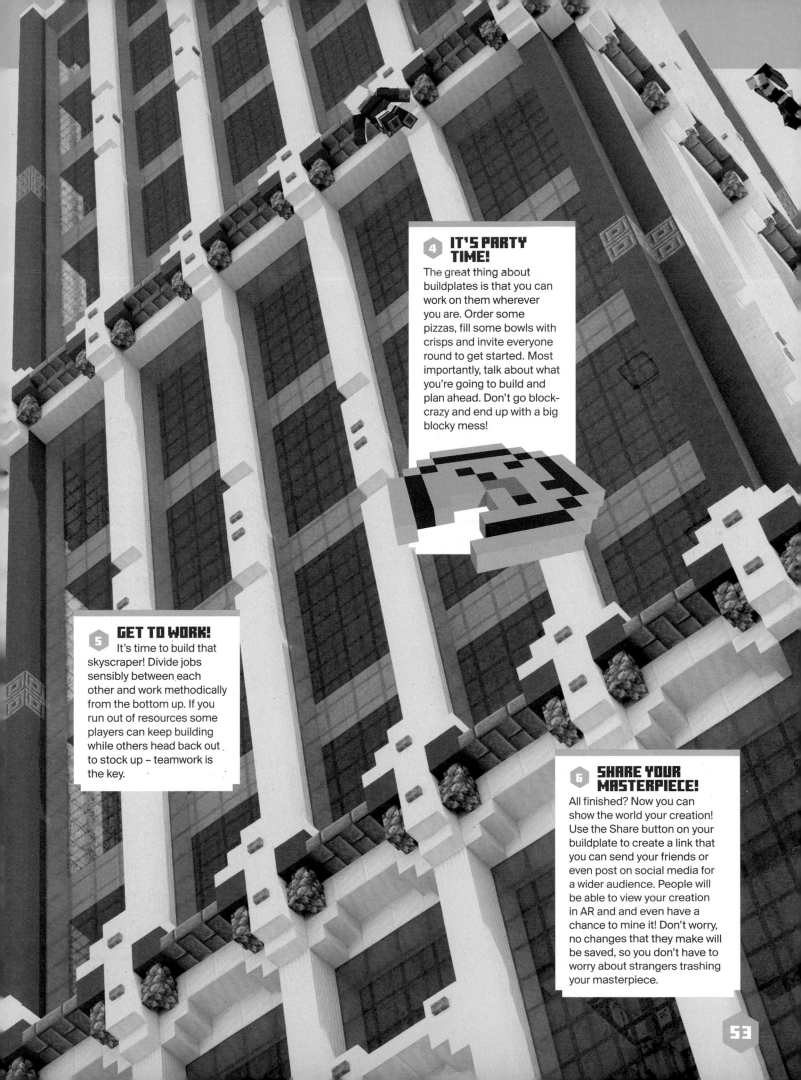

4 IT'S PARTY TIME!

The great thing about buildplates is that you can work on them wherever you are. Order some pizzas, fill some bowls with crisps and invite everyone round to get started. Most importantly, talk about what you're going to build and plan ahead. Don't go block-crazy and end up with a big blocky mess!

5 GET TO WORK!

It's time to build that skyscraper! Divide jobs sensibly between each other and work methodically from the bottom up. If you run out of resources some players can keep building while others head back out to stock up – teamwork is the key.

6 SHARE YOUR MASTERPIECE!

All finished? Now you can show the world your creation! Use the Share button on your buildplate to create a link that you can send your friends or even post on social media for a wider audience. People will be able to view your creation in AR and and even have a chance to mine it! Don't worry, no changes that they make will be saved, so you don't have to worry about strangers trashing your masterpiece.

BUILDERS & BIOMES

It's finally out! Are you as excited to play Builders and Biomes as I am? Full of skeletons, zombies and creepers, I couldn't wait to take my favourite video game to the tabletop! In Builders and Biomes, players are sent out into the Overworld to mine resources, build structures and gain experience points. Sounds familiar, right? Let's take a look at the game!

BOARD GAMES WITH MONTY

GAMEPLAY

So what is Builders and Biomes? Well, just like in Minecraft, it's a game where each player sets out to gather resources and survive in the Overworld. Players will face challenges along the way, collecting experience points for structures built and mobs defeated. The game ends when three level of blocks in the block stack are removed. The player with the most points at the end of the game wins!

YOUR TURN

On your turn, you can take 2 different actions:
- Collect 2 blocks
- Move 0-2 spaces and reveal cards
- Build structure
- Fight mob
- Collect weapon

BLOCK STACK

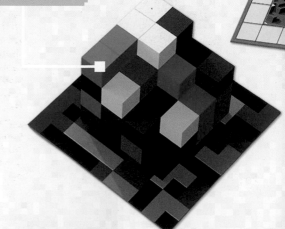

SPECIAL MOVES

Battling mobs is a big part of Minecraft, and that hasn't changed in Builders and Biomes. Take a close look at your attack cards. Some of them have special moves that can give you an edge in the fight.

BIOMES

Players will have the option of venturing into each of their favourite biomes – forests, deserts, mountains and snowy tundra – and are encouraged to collect weapons, fight mobs and, of course, build their favourite structures.

PLAYTESTING

It took five prototypes to develop the concept for Builder's and Biomes. Some concepts were too easy, some were too complex. This edition is the perfect balance between the two. What are you waiting for? Go show your friends how to play!

HURDLES

Being a block-based game, Builders & Biomes was originally going to be all about blocks. It quickly became clear that it would be very tricky to make this a reality – playing a 4-player game with 50 blocks simply wouldn't work. So, the developers scratched their heads and became even more creative. The result? An extremely enjoyable board game!

VARIANT FOR BEGINNERS

Playing board games involves learning lots of new rules. If you are playing for the first time, or with young children, you can use simplified rules to make it easier to play. Simplify the scoring rounds by counting player spaces on the board. This will also make the game easier as you can now place the building cards on any space of your player board for the same number of points.

DEVELOPER INSIGHT

Curious how a video game can be transformed into a tabletop board game? We asked the game developer himself, Ulrich Blum. Ulrich had this insight to share;

'The first thing I did was play Minecraft non-stop for about a week'

Hey, I wonder if he needs help with the next edition. My box-shaped eyes are testament to the many non-stop weeks I've played.

MINECRAFT: HOUR OF CODE

Have you ever dreamed of making your own game? With Minecraft: Hour of Code you can learn the basics of coding with the game you love! The Hour of Code scheme provides introductory lessons to computer science using Minecraft. Coding can nurture problem solving skills, logic and creativity. Head over to the Hour of Code website to find out what else you can learn.

CHALLENGE TIME WITH MONTY

FOREST FIRE

A forest fire is threatening to burn down a village and it's up to you to save the day. Program your coding assistant, the Agent, to navigate the forest and collect data about fires. Then write code to help prevent the spread of the fire, save the village and bring life back to the forest.

WHAT IS CODING?

Coding is giving a computer a series of instructions to complete a task. It's just like following a recipe! Easy right? Today, we're going to look at coding artificial intelligence, known as AI.

WHAT IS ARTIFICIAL INTELLIGENCE ?

AI is the ability a computer has to think and learn, and it can be used in many different ways. The team at Hour of Code have been inspired by AI's potential to deal with environmental crises, cure disease and generally improve our way of life. They've created a very special lesson for Minecraft environmentalists around the world – how to use AI to prevent forest fires. Forests help ensure clean air, fresh water and sustain life for over half the world's species. In this lesson, we're going to learn the basics of coding and AI while tackling forest fires in the world of Minecraft. Give it a go!

MICROSOFT: AI FOR EARTH

Interested in finding out more about AI and how we can use technology as a force for positive change? Head over to Microsoft and read all about their amazing AI For Earth project that uses AI to solve global environmental challenges.

JAVASCRIPT

Minecraft is coded in a programming language known as JavaScript. Did you know that many of your favourite websites and minigames are created in JavaScript?

① MINECRAFT: EDUCATION EDITION

To access the lesson, simply download Minecraft: Education Edition from Minecraft.net to your device and then launch the program. When you're ready to begin, press Play to start the lesson. It's available in 20 languages and is absolutely free.

AI FOR GOOD CHALLENGE

Learn the basics of coding with Minecraft Education: AI for Good. In this Hour of Code lesson, you'll learn how to code artificial intelligence by saving a local village from a raging forest fire. Are you ready to learn how to use AI for good? Download Minecraft: Education Edition to get started.

2 FOLLOW THE INSTRUCTIONS ON SCREEN TO NAVIGATE TO THE FIRST TASK

Use your mouse and movement buttons to navigate in your desired direction. When you reach a non-player character (NPC), right-click on the NPC to get information on how to continue on your quest.

4 HELP AGENT COMPLETE THE TASKS

Now that you know the basics, it's time to meet Agent, your robot coding sidekick! Continue following the lesson plan to learn how to code AI to prevent forest fires.

5 HELP A NEARBY VILLAGE

You have been tasked with helping a nearby village prevent a forest fire. Using your new coding knowledge and with the help of your coding assistant Agent, write some code to put out the fire. When you're done, take it a step further and teach Agent to replant seeds in the area.

3 CODE BUILDER

Press the C key to open the Code Builder screen and start coding. To build your code, drag and drop the code blocks into your desired order and press play to run the code.

HELPER BOT

If you get stuck, ask the Helper Bot to reset the task. After attempting to complete an activity, you can choose to try again or skip to the next lesson. You must attempt the task before you skip it!

PARKOUR PARK BUILD CHALLENGE

PART 1

BUILDING
WITH SPARKS

Parkour maps demand precise movement and buckets of bravery to complete. Are you up to the challenge of designing your own? Your mates will be amazed when you invite them to leap and hop their way through your fiendish creation. Ready? Get building!

1 BALANCING ACT!

Connect the different sections of your parkour park using twisty-turny raised fences. Players will have to balance high in the air as they jump from fence to fence. Don't look down!

2 THIRSTING FOR ADVENTURE!

Place potion dispensers near the start containing potions of leaping II and potions of swiftness II so that everyone has the required sprinting and jumping boosts to really go for it!

3 UPS AND DOWNS!

Don't just require players to constantly move upwards. Alternate between raised and lowered platforms. You want to keep people on their toes.

4 CHOOSE A STYLE!

Give your park a distinctive theme or look. Is it a slippery snowy map, or a jungle course where players must jump from tree to tree? If you really want to scare people, go for a fiery theme and make the floor lava.

5 FREESTYLE OR NOT?

How do you want people to play? A linear obstacle course is best if you want to run time trial races, but an open map that lets people choose how to get across offers more variety and replay value. Which playstyle do you prefer?

6 ADD VARIETY!

A parkour map that is just lots of jumping from block to block will soon get boring. Mix things up by requiring different ways of moving. Make players jump onto ladders, swim across pools and trundle down rails.

PARKOUR PARK BUILD CHALLENGE

PART 2

I FEEL SICK!

A line of pistons, all set to open and close at different speeds, will really test your players' balance. Follow the guide to create your very own parkour piston feature. What devilish combinations can you come up with?

A STICKY SITUATION!

You don't need to be a creepy crawly spider to stick to walls in Minecraft! Use honey blocks to build wall runs that players can use to cross larger gaps in style. Just remember that you can't jump from a honey block, so design your wall accordingly.

KA-BOING!

Use slime block trampolines to make your park even more fun. How high a player bounces off a slime block depends on how far they fell onto it, so test it yourself and make sure players have somewhere safe to land.

PUMP IT UP!

Jumping on normal blocks is all very well, but why not spice up your parkour park with moving parts? Repeating redstone pistons are easy to build and a great way to add additional peril. Follow this guide to build very own clock circuit piston wall for your parkour park.

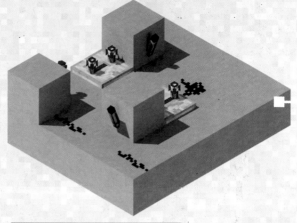

1 Start by building a clock circuit. This redstone mechanism will continue to produce a signal until you switch it off.

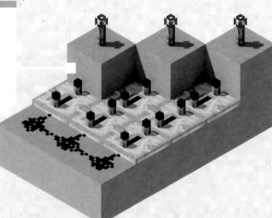

2 Then build a timing mechanism. Decide how fast you want your pistons to go in and out by setting the ticks to your desired speed.

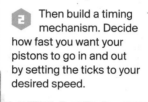

3 Build a signal ladder to your pistons. This can be as tall as you like – just use blocks and redstone torches between your redstone repeaters and pistons.

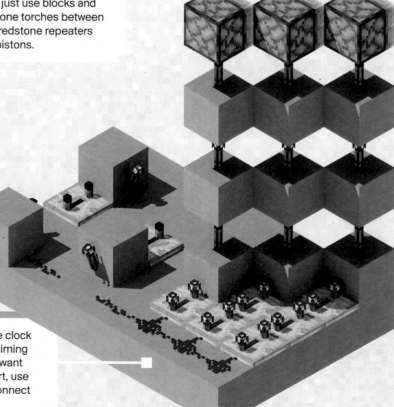

4 Lastly, join the clock circuit to the timing mechanism. If you want to space them apart, use redstone dust to connect the circuits.

THE COOLEST COMMUNITY

One of the best things about Minecraft is how it reaches out into the real world, bringing people together and helping to make positive changes. There are always countless events happening around the world, from small gatherings to huge international conventions. Here are some of our favourites ...

EXPERT GUIDE
WITH SCOUT

WELL IMPRESSIVE!

The Village & Pillage update brought new well systems to Minecraft, and Mojang celebrated by supporting charity Water's Weekend for Water fundraising drive. Some of the internet's top stars, including JackSepticEye, teamed up with their fans on shared projects and together raised over $117,000 to bring clean drinking water to some of the world's poorest people.

NETHER MEANT

Have you ever attended a virtual concert? Last April, event producers Open Pit and Anamanaguchi joined forces to throw a Minecraft-based benefit concert for COVID-19. Listeners could attend the concert in-game and see stars such as Baths, Wavedash, Hana and headliner American Football perform in an accurate recreation of Brooklyn's hot club Elsewhere.

MINECON 2019

Minecrafters around the world were glued to this livestreamed community event from Nashville, USA which revealed loads of cool new features coming to the game. Away from the main video feed there were also live panels with top modders and builders, and the whole event was hosted by Mojang's very own Lydia Winters with help from YouTubers Masuo, Marielitai, Shubble and Dangthatsalongname. All told, over 5.5 million people tuned in to watch! Simply staggering!

MINECRAFT LIVE 2020
Minecraft Live is filmed live and beamed across the world via the internet! It will happen this fall; packed with exciting Minecraft announcements and news, demos, community creators, and will include pre and post show bits, as well as on-demand panels.

BUILD AND WIN!

Congratulations to French teenager Louis Varin, who won a national contest in October 2019 to design a sustainable town in Minecraft. Louis' creation was chosen because it encouraged biodiversity, saved water, reduced energy use, and improved the quality of life of its imaginary inhabitants. Bravo, Louis! The 16-year-old beat over 1,200 other entries to win and received a 3D-printed model of his town as a prize. Why not see if there are any Minecraft contests you could enter?

CODING TUTORIALS

Hour of Code, the team that brought us the AI for Good tutorial, have been busy with the release of the latest tutorial in their series of coding classes for young budding programmers, Minecraft Voyage Aquatic. In this tutorial series, players learn and develop the basics of coding while creating their very own game. Visit their website to find out more, starting with Minecraft Adventurer and Minecraft Designer.

CAMPFIRE TALES

The community never fails to impress and inspire me! Every day new stories are told of how loving and caring the community is. Here are some stories of wild adventures, wonderful people and epic builds from across the many realms of Minecraft!

EXPERT GUIDE
WITH SPARKS

A LOVING TRIBUTE

One of the greatest things about Minecraft is how it brings people together, and few people embodied that more than Bryan "Pendar2" Heffernan. Back in 2011, Brian created the incredibly popular Emenbee server, which went on to host over a million players. Sadly, Bryan became terminally ill with cancer and had to close the server. Soon after, the server was revived by friends and fans who wanted to pay tribute to Brian and to all he had done for the Minecraft community. Thousands of players logged in commemorate his memory.

A KALEIDOSCOPIC WORLD!

This might just be the most crazy and colourful build we've ever seen! It's called Authenticity Relocated, and was built by environment artist Immanuel I. M. K. Designed to be truly alien and dreamlike, the map features lots of gravity-defying structures like flying trees and jellyfish hovering above brightly coloured terrain. Immanuel describes it as "a reality that has taken root in an entirely alien genre" and we couldn't agree more! If you're looking for a map suitable for truly weird adventures, this is the one!

A LEGEND FINALLY FALLS!

Phil "Ph1LzA" Watson's unbroken five-year game of Hardcore Survival Mode was abruptly brought to an end in April 2019. Phil walked 6,316km, flew 7,798km and jumped 732,389 times during his record-breaking run but after being startled by a baby zombie, shot by a skeleton and finally chomped by a spider, his character finally died during a live Twitch stream. His incredible story was featured by the BBC and national newspapers and he's since put his fame to good use, raising money for the Red Cross online. We salute you, Ph1LzA!

NATION BUILDING!

What's the biggest thing you've ever made? A building? A village? A whole city? Step aside for IGFredMcWaffe who spent six years building an entire country! It's called *The Republic of Union Islands* and features six distinct states within its borders. Each state has its own architecture and culture, and Fred has even worked out a complete history for the country as well as working out where in the real world it would be (close to New Zealand, in case you were wondering). And the most amazing part is ... he's still adding more to it! Truly epic!

DECIPHER THE ILLAGER

Become a master codebreaker! Bear has escaped the Arch-Illager's lands with encrypted notes. You must crack the code and reveal what they say. Study the arcane glyphs and cryptic runes in the book below and use the cipher to decrypt the hidden message.

CHALLENGE
TIME
WITH BEAR

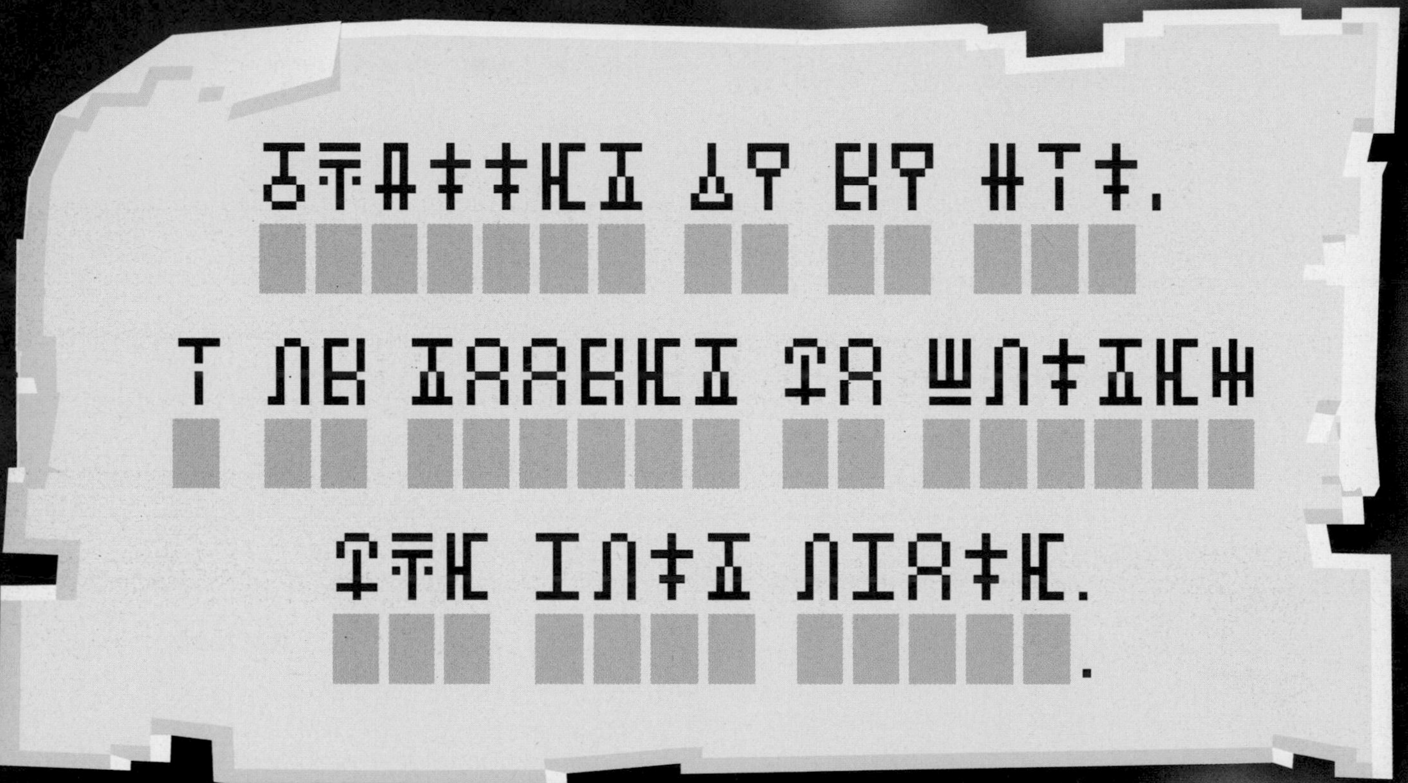

KEY
A B C D E F G H I J K L M
N O P Q R S T U V W X Y Z

GOODBYE

Wow, what a year!

As we sprint further into our next decade of Minecraft's history, it just keeps getting bigger and bigger. But we'll never forget it's all down to you and your amazing creativity.

Thank you so much for playing!

Alex Wiltshire Mojang

ANSWERS

20-21

66-67

SHUNNED BY MY KIN, I AM DOOMED TO WANDER THE LAND ALONE.

AT LONG LAST, I HAVE FOUND SOMETHING THAT WILL CHANGE MY FUTURE FOREVER, THE ORB OF DOMINANCE.

ALL SHALL BOW BEFORE ME! AND THOSE WHO DO NOT BOW, SHALL FALL.